THE VALUE OF CREATIVITY

The Story of Thomas Edison

VALUE COMMUNICATIONS, INC.
PUBLISHERS
LA JOLLA, CALIFORNIA

THE VALUE OF CREATIVITY

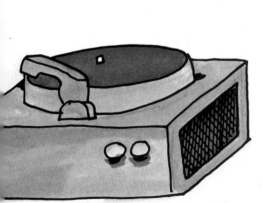

The Story of
Thomas Edison

BY ANN DONEGAN JOHNSON

The Value of Creativity is part of the ValueTales series.

The Value of Creativity text copyright © 1981 by Ann Donegan Johnson. Illustrations copyright © 1981 by Value Communications, Inc.

First Edition
Manufactured in the United States of America

For information write to:
Value Communications, Inc.
P.O. Box 1012
La Jolla, California 92038

Library of Congress Cataloging in Publication Data

Johnson, Ann Donegan.
   The value of creativity — the story of Thomas Edison.

   (The ValueTales)
   SUMMARY: A biography of one of history's most prolific inventors, stressing his ingenuity and creativity.
   1. Edison, Thomas Alva, 1847-1931 — Juvenile literature.
2. Inventors — United States — Biography — Juvenile literature. [1. Edison, Thomas Alva, 1847-1931. 2. Inventors.
3. Creative ability]
I. Pileggi, Steve. II. Title.
        TK140.E3J63   621.3″092″4 [B] [92]   80-28152
ISBN 0-916392-72-4

1 2 3 4 5 6 7 8 9 84 83 82 81

This tale is about a very creative person, Thomas Edison. The story that follows is based on events in his life. More historical facts about Thomas Edison can be found on page 63.

Once upon a time...

more than a hundred years ago, a little boy named Thomas Alva Edison lived with his parents in the small town of Milan, Ohio.

Tom was a lively child. Perhaps he was *too* lively. He was always taking things apart and putting them together again — or trying to put them together.

"Good night!" said his father one day. "Look at this! Another broken toy!"

"Now don't be hard on him," said his mother. "He only wants to see how things work."

But one day even Tom's mother lost her patience. That was the day Tom decided to find out what would happen if he kindled a little fire in the corner of the barn.

What happened was that the barn caught fire. Tom's neighbors came running with buckets of water to put out the blaze, and Tom trembled.

"I'm really in for it now!" he thought.

8

Indeed Tom was in for it. The next day Tom's father marched the boy down to the village square. There, in front of all the townspeople, Mr. Edison gave Tom a thorough whipping.

"No!" cried Tom. "Please stop! That's enough!"

"I'll decide when you've had enough!" shouted Mr. Edison. "I'll see that you remember this for a long, long time!"

Tom did remember the whipping. He never forgot it. But he didn't let it stop him from taking things apart to see how they worked. He didn't let it stop him from trying to do things in new ways.

"He's a creative little fellow, isn't he?" said a neighbor, after Tom's mother found him sitting on a nest in the neighbor's barn, trying to hatch some geese from the eggs he had found there.

His mother laughed. "It's always interesting," she said. "I only wish he didn't get into so much trouble."

One day Tom came home to find his parents in the parlor. His father looked very serious, and his mother was dabbing at her eyes with her apron.

''Mother, you're crying!'' said Tom. ''What's the matter?''

''Your mother is a bit upset, Tom,'' said his father. ''I've just told her that we'll have to move. I did hope that the railroad would come to Milan and business would pick up, but that isn't going to happen. No one is building new houses, and I can't make enough money to keep my lumber mill open.''

Tom felt a strange heaviness inside himself when he heard this. "Move?" said he. "Move where? Where will we go?"

"To Port Huron, Michigan," said Mr. Edison. "I can get work there."

Tom knew there was no point in arguing. His father had to make a living. Just the same, Tom felt lonely. He would have to leave the only home he had ever known. He would have to say goodbye to all of his friends.

"I wish I could take just one playmate with me," he whispered to himself. "Or a pet! Maybe if I had a pet it would help."

Tom shut his eyes and tried to imagine that he did have a pet — a fluffy dog with long ears and a waggly tail.

And when Tom opened his eyes, there was the dog!

"Oh, boy!" cried Tom. "Am I dreaming, or are you really there?"

"Well now," said the dog. "Let's say that I'm here as long as you believe I'm here. It's up to you. You imagined me, didn't you? You dreamed me up out of nothing. I guess we could say you created me."

"You can talk!" said Tom. "Hey, that's great! I'm going to call you Sparkey. Sparkey Watts. Do you like that?"

"Not bad," said the dog. "At least it's more original than Rover or Spot. Now what's all this about being lonely in Port Huron? Don't you know that things won't be so different there? You can take all the really important things with you. You can take your imagination and your creativity. And you can take me!"

Tom knew that this was true. He knew, too, that when Sparkey Watts talked to him that way, it was really his own good sense talking. He cheered up immediately, and he helped his mother pack for the move. When he got to Port Huron, he helped her unpack again in the big white house near the lake.

"This won't be bad at all," said Tom to Sparkey. "Look how close we are to the water. I can go fishing every day."

"Not quite," said his mother. "You're a big boy now, Tom. It's time you went to school."

The next day, Mrs. Edison took Tom to the school that was run by the Reverend Engle and his wife. There Tom was told to sit still on a hard bench and to pay attention. He was also told that he would have to memorize dates and place names and words in the spelling lessons and sums in the arithmetic book.

"This is terrible!" said Tom to himself. "I don't think I can learn anything this way."

Tom began to wriggle and fidget in his seat. He let his imagination roam free. He pictured himself and his little make-believe friend, Sparkey Watts, racing through the fields and swimming in the lake.

When the Reverend Engle called on Tom to recite, Tom didn't answer. He was so busy daydreaming that he hadn't even heard his teacher.

"That boy is completely addled," said the Reverend Engle, after Tom had been in his school for three months.

Tom heard that, and he didn't like it. He got up and ran out of the school and back to his own home.

"Addled?" said Mrs. Edison, when she heard what had happened. "Nobody is going to call my boy addled. From now on he'll stay home and I'll teach him myself!"

Tom's mother worked with him for hours each day, and she taught him to love reading. Tom was nine when his parents gave him a copy of *Parker's Natural and Experimental Philosophy.* It was a book about science, and Tom thought it was marvelous. He decided immediately that he would be a scientist, and he set up a laboratory in his basement.

"What's he doing down there?" demanded his father one day. "It can't be good for a growing boy to spend all his time in a dark, damp cellar."

"I know," said his mother. "It does worry me a little. You never know what he's up to. Of course he's clever and original and . . . and . . ."

"Don't tell me," said his father. "He's creative!"

No sooner were the words out of Mr. Edison's mouth than there was an explosion in the cellar that fairly rocked the house!

"I was making a cannon," said Tom, when his mother and father came dashing to the top of the cellar stairs.

"Tell me again how creative he is," said Mr. Edison to Tom's mother.

"Tom, stop that this minute!" scolded Mrs. Edison. "Not another cannon ever, do you understand?"

So Tom gave up his attempt to create firearms, and he decided to experiment with static electricity instead.

''Cats have lots of static electricity in their fur,'' he said to Sparkey. ''Sometimes they give off sparks when you stroke them. Now if I fasten two cats together with wire and then . . .''

''Don't do it!'' warned Sparkey.

But Tom did find two tomcats, and he did attach wires to them. Then he tried to rub their tails together.

The cats suddenly became hissing, screaming, scratching whirlwinds of fur.

Tom and Sparkey ran for their lives!

"That wasn't too smart," said Sparkey, when they stopped running at last.

"You never know till you try," said Tom cheerfully.

"Yes, you do," said Sparkey. "With cats, you know! Cats don't like to be handled that way!"

But Tom wasn't listening. Tom had spotted his friend Michael Oates. Michael was strolling down the street whistling. He looked like a boy with time on his hands.

"Michael!" called Tom. "Have you ever wanted to fly?"

"To fly?" Michael blinked and thought about this. "I guess it would be fun," he said.

"I've been reading about the way balloons go up in the air," said Tom. "They fly because they're full of gas. Now if you took a bunch of Seidlitz powders, you'd have lots of gas in your stomach. Then maybe you'd be able to fly, just like a balloon."

Michael looked doubtful, but he trailed after Tom toward the basement laboratory.

"I have a feeling this isn't going to work worth a darn," said Sparkey Watts, and he trotted along behind the boys.

Sparkey was right. Michael took the Seidlitz powders and he didn't fly. He ran home with a stomach ache, and Tom got a spanking from his mother.

"All right," said Tom, when the excitement had died down. "So it didn't work. Not everything does. But I've been reading about a new invention called the telegraph. I'm going to build a telegraph, and I'll bet it *will* work!"

"Great!" said Sparkey Watts, "but this time, try to figure out what you're doing before you do it. You'll need to know about electricity — and I don't mean the kind you make by rubbing two cats together!"

Tom knew that Sparkey Watts was right. He got all the books he could find about electricity, and he began to study. When he felt that he understood the subject, he set to work, together with his friend Jim Clancy.

The boys strung wires on the trees from Tom's house to Jim's. They got batteries and electromagnets and all sorts of gear, and when everything was ready, each boy went to his own house. Tom tapped at the telegraph key and Jim heard the long and short noises of the code. Tom was tapping out the word, "Hello!"

"Wonderful!" said Sparkey Watts. "And you'll notice that nothing exploded — not even once!"

When he was twelve, Tom heard that there was a job opening on the train that ran from Port Huron to Detroit, Michigan. The trainmen needed a boy to sell candy and sandwiches to the passengers.

"Mother, can I go?" said Tom. "I can make money to help you and Dad, and I'll have some left over to buy chemicals and equipment for my laboratory."

Mrs. Edison frowned. "You're too young," she said. "Besides, you'll fall behind in your lessons."

"No I won't," declared Tom. "I'll study on the train while we're in the station in Detroit."

"Let him do it," said Mr. Edison. "He's big enough. It won't hurt him to get out and help earn his keep."

So it was settled. Two days later, Tom was at the station at seven in the morning. He had a huge basket piled high with food and magazines and newspapers.

When the train pulled out of the station, Tom walked through the cars with his basket. "Candy!" he called out. "Magazines! Nuts! Sandwiches!"

"Here, boy!" cried a passenger.

"I'll have a sandwich!" said a second passenger.

Tom's food and his magazines and newspapers were soon sold, and he could sit and read the science book he had brought from home.

"That should make your mother happy," said Sparkey. "What are you reading about now? And what new experiments are you going to try when you get home?"

"I'm not sure," said Tom, "but they'll be experiments nobody's ever tried before!"

Before long, Tom began doing experiments in the half-empty baggage car aboard the train. He fixed a workbench there, and he brought his chemicals from home so that he could go on with his own work when he wasn't busy peddling sandwiches and candy.

One day Tom was late getting to the station. The train was ready to
pull out, and Tom had to run with his arms full of newspapers.

The train began to move, and Tom put out a hand and grabbed at the
railing next to the steps of the last car. He caught it, but he couldn't
pull himself up.

"Hang on!" cried the conductor. "I'll help you!"

He reached down, caught Tom by the ears and pulled him aboard the train.

Tom stood on the platform of the train and shook his head. His ears were ringing, and in a few seconds they began to hurt. He could see that the conductor was talking to him, but he could not hear what the man said.

Tom had always had trouble with earaches and colds, and now the tug the conductor had given him had really damaged his ears. He was beginning to go deaf!

Soon Tom was unable to hear the birds sing. He could not hear his friends when they laughed together. He tried not to be unhappy, and he filled the growing silence with reading, with experiments in his laboratory, with peddling his wares on the train, and with his new venture — a newspaper.

Tom had seen that newspapers were very important to his customers, and he decided to publish his own paper. He bought an old printing press and put it into the baggage car near his workbench. His newspaper, the *Grand Trunk Herald,* was the first newspaper ever published aboard a train.

Tom thought publishing was great fun, and before long he went into partnership with a young friend who worked at the newspaper in Port Huron. The two decided to put out a gossip sheet called *Paul Pry*.

"Tom, be careful," warned Sparkey. "Gossip can be dangerous. Once it starts, you have no way of telling how it will end."

But Tom and his friend were too excited to be careful, and their new paper was popular from the start. People bought it so that they could chuckle when they read the little stories about their neighbors.

Of course Tom and his friend didn't print people's names. They really didn't want to harm anyone, and they only used initials. But when they printed an item that said that a young man named F. had better keep out of J. W.'s saloon, a doctor in Port Huron thought they were writing about his son.

"Where's the editor?" cried the doctor, bursting into the place where Tom and his friend were setting type for the next edition of their paper. "Wait till I get my hands on him! I'll throw him in the lake!"

Of course Tom didn't say that *he* was the editor. He didn't say much of anything. But when the doctor had stormed away, he decided that in the future he would be more careful. "You were right," he told Sparkey. "Gossip is dangerous. It may have hurt that man's son — and it surely could have hurt me!"

Tom eventually lost interest in his newspaper, but he never lost interest in his experiments. He kept working in his traveling laboratory until the day the train bumped over a rough spot on the track, and some jars tumbled off a high shelf and crashed onto the floor.

"Tom, watch out!" cried Sparkey.

One of the jars had contained phosphorus, and it burst into flames.

"What's going on here?" cried the conductor as he rushed into the baggage car.

Tom didn't answer. He was busy trying to put the fire out. The conductor pitched in and helped him, and they beat down the flames.

When the train reached the next stop, the conductor heaved Tom's workbench and his collection of chemicals out the door.

"Don't ever let me see any of those bottles on my train again!" he shouted.

After that Tom did his experimenting at home in Port Huron. When he had time to spare on the train, he read or he napped.

Sometimes when the train stopped at Mount Clemens, Michigan, he got off and talked with Mr. MacKenzie, who ran the telegraph office there.

One day Tom swung off the train and saw that Mr. MacKenzie's little boy had wandered onto the railroad tracks. A boxcar was rolling toward the child. Tom raced to scoop the boy off the tracks and out of the way of the rolling car.

Mr. MacKenzie was so grateful that he hardly knew how to thank Tom. "Perhaps I could teach you telegraphy," he said. "Would you like to learn?"

"You bet I would!" said Tom. From then on he left the train every day at Mount Clemens, and he learned to send and receive on Mr. MacKenzie's telegraph instruments.

Tom was sixteen when he got his first real job. He was made a night telegrapher and station agent. The job was across the Canadian border in Stratford, Ontario.

Tom wasn't working in Stratford long before he had trouble. He had developed the habit of taking catnaps on the train, and now he found that he couldn't stay awake all night.

"Maybe it would help if you slept in the daytime," said Sparkey.

"Don't be silly," said Tom. "I have to read in the daytime, and study, and work on my experiments." And Tom rigged up one of his first practical inventions. It was a device that would send a signal to his boss every half hour. Even if Tom dropped off to sleep, the signal would go out and the boss would think that Tom was awake and alert.

But sleeping on the job is a serious matter — especially for someone who is a station agent and a telegrapher. Tom's boss discovered what was happening, and Tom's days in Stratford were over.

For the next few years Tom wandered about from city to city. Telegraph operators were needed everywhere, and Tom could usually find work. However, he couldn't hold onto a job very long. He was too interested in reading and experimenting and sketching and planning. He wanted to create new inventions — to build things that no one had thought of before. He would neglect to take down incoming messages, or he would let outgoing messages pile up. Then suddenly he would be out of work once again.

"Being creative is very nice," said Sparkey at last, "but there's nothing wrong with eating, either. Do you suppose you could manage to pay attention for a while so that we could get some money ahead?"

"All right," said Tom. "I'll pay attention and we'll go to Boston. That's the center for scientific learning. I can work there and keep up with things that are going on in the world of science. Maybe I'll create something that's really needed."

"Maybe," said Sparkey. "Up till now you've just been amusing yourself. You know that, don't you?"

Tom didn't like to admit this, but he knew it was true. He took Sparkey's words to heart, and when he reached Boston he got a job as a telegrapher for Western Union. For a while he did pay attention, and things went better than they usually did.

After a while, however, Tom decided that a job wasn't really what he should have. "What I should really do is make a fortune," he said. "Then I wouldn't have to worry about jobs at all."

"A lovely idea, but is it practical?" said Sparkey.

"We'll soon find out," said Tom, and he set to work on an invention that he believed was really necessary.

It was an automatic vote recorder, and Tom planned to persuade members of Congress to use it. Then, instead of taking the time to stand and vote "Aye" or "Nay" on the measures that were submitted to Congress, the lawmakers in Washington could simply flip a switch at their desks, and their votes would be recorded at the desk of the speaker.

"They're bound to like it," said Tom, when his recorder was ready. "Look how efficient it is! The entire Congress can vote in just a few minutes!"

Tom quit his job and went to Washington. And were the legislators interested in his invention?

They were not. They didn't care whether they were efficient or not. They sent Tom on his way, as lean and hungry as ever.

Sparkey and Tom went to New York, and Tom happened to be at the gold exchange the day the indicator broke down.

The gold indicator was much like the stock ticker we know today. A sort of telegraph sent out information on gold prices to the offices of brokers all over New York. One day the indicator broke and the tickers began to run wild. In no time, people crowded into the gold room, shouting "Fix the machine! Fix it! Fix it!"

No one could do this until Tom Edison stepped forward. In just an hour or two he had the indicator running perfectly --again.

At last Tom's talents were appreciated.

In the months that followed, Tom improved the gold indicators. He invented a device that would stop all the ticker machines in the brokerage offices if the central transmitter should break down again. "This way there won't be such a panic," he told Sparkey.

The officials of the indicator company were delighted with Tom's creation. They were happy to pay him $40,000 for his invention.

"My stars!" said Sparkey, as they hurried to the bank with the check. "I've never seen so much money in all my life. What are you going to do with it, Tom?"

"I'm going to go into business for myself," Tom declared. "I'll never have to worry about jobs and bosses again!"

And Tom, who was just twenty-three years old, opened a workshop and laboratory in Newark, New Jersey. He began to hire assistants to help him.

''I want to fix things so that the world can run on electricity,'' Tom told Sparkey. ''It will be a big job, and I can't do it alone!''

It was just at this time that Tom met a very pretty girl named Mary Stilwell. She worked at the Gold & Stock Company punching perforations into telegraph tape.

Once he had seen her, Tom himself did very little work. Instead he haunted the Gold & Stock Company. He stood near Mary and stared at her with admiration.

The other employees laughed when they saw Tom, and they teased Mary about him. She was flustered and embarrassed.

One day, when this had been going on for some time, Tom went to Mary and said, rather bluntly, "Will you marry me?"

Mary was only sixteen. She was startled and almost frightened. She didn't know how to answer. However, she did like this bright, creative young man, and on Christmas Day in 1871, the two were married.

The day after his marriage, Tom was back at work, and in the years that followed there was a great explosion of creative energy. Tom was constantly designing devices that would improve telegraphy. He also improved the telephone which Alexander Graham Bell had invented.

In 1876, when he was twenty-nine, Edison moved his workshop from Newark to Menlo Park, New Jersey. At Menlo Park he announced that he was working on a talking machine.

"You mean you're going to save us the trouble of talking for ourselves?" laughed one of Edison's assistants.

The man soon learned what Tom meant. He watched Tom wrap tinfoil around the cylinder on a strange little machine. Then Tom turned a crank on the machine and began to recite, "Mary had a little lamb, its fleece was white as snow."

As Tom recited, a pointed instrument moved on the machine, and when Tom stopped reciting and turned the machine back to its starting place, the assistant heard Tom's voice again. This time it came from the machine.

Tom had invented the phonograph, and it was to become one of his most beloved creations.

But it was not the phonograph for which Thomas Alva Edison is best known. It was his invention of a new kind of electric light that really changed the world.

Until Tom figured out how to make them, there were no light bulbs like the ones we use today. For all the time before then, people had only the glow from fireplaces, candles, oil or gas lamps, or other open flames to give light at night and to brighten dark places.

Tom Edison began working on this great invention in 1878. When he started, he knew that he and his helpers had a very difficult problem to solve.

"We have to find a way to use electricity to make a lamp that will glow but won't melt or burn up," he told his staff of dedicated assistants.

"Golly," said Sparkey Watts. "Are you sure you even want to try this one?"

"Remember, Tom" Sparkey went on, "many famous scientists, people who know all about how light and electricity work, have tried to make such a lamp — and none of them could do it. Maybe you should read what they have written about this very difficult problem before you spend a lot of time and money on experiments that might not work."

"That could just get in my way," said Tom. "When I start on an invention, I don't read books. I don't want to know what has already been done. I start from scratch."

Tom didn't know all the rules about light and electricity that the scientists knew. But he did know that to create something brand new you had to work long and hard. He knew you had to try all sorts of new ways to do something no one had ever done before — that was the secret of coming up with a great invention; that was the secret of creativity.

And in the months that followed, Tom Edison and his helpers worked very hard indeed. They worked day and night. When they were exhausted, they curled up on tables and in chairs to snatch a few winks of sleep. Then they woke to work some more.

Tom knew their task involved several problems. The new kind of lamp would need a glass globe to hold the light. They had to find a way to make the globe strong enough so it wouldn't shatter. Tom even hired a skilled glass blower from Germany to make better globes. They also had to make special pumps to draw the air from the globes, because the part of the new lamp that glowed — the filament — would burn up in air.

Finally, Tom knew the most important thing was finding just the right material for the filament of his new light. And that was the hardest part.

Tom and his assistants tried all sorts of filaments. One after another, they were inserted into the glass globes — and one after another, when the electricity heated the filaments to make them glow, they burned up or melted, or the globes exploded.

In 1879 — after months of labor and thousands of experiments — Tom Edison found a thin carbon filament that worked. He had succeeded in creating a lamp that glowed with a steady, bright, long-lasting light.

His creativity had produced a new kind of light — called incandescent light — in which a current of electricity passed through a fine filament inside a glass globe and gave off lots of light, but little heat.

After inventing his great new lamp, Tom went on to perfect an entire electrical system — generators, wiring, fuses, sockets — everything that would make it possible for people everywhere to have his electric lights.

At the end of 1879, Tom presented his invention to the world.

Crowds flocked to Menlo Park to see the lights on the streets and lanes near Edison's laboratory. They were awed by the spectacle, and some predicted that the world would never be the same again. They called Edison the Wizard of Menlo Park, and soon kings and presidents and other famous and distinguished people were heaping honors on him.

No doubt this pleased Edison. It would please anyone. But what pleased him even more was the knowledge that he had accomplished something really worthwhile, using only his creativity, his energy of mind, and his determination.

Perhaps you are like Edison. Perhaps you always try new things, or you think of new ways of doing old things. Perhaps you like to make things up out of your head, using your own original ideas.

Of course there isn't anything wrong with doing things the old way — the sure way that always works — but when you try new ways, there is always a chance that they will turn out to be better ways. And if you try them, you may have more fun and you may create wonderful things, too.

Just like our good friend, Thomas Edison.

The End

Thomas Alva Edison, the greatest and most prolific inventor of his time, was born in Milan, Ohio, in 1847. He was the youngest child of Samuel and Nancy Elliott Edison. His mother had been a schoolteacher, and she was determined that Thomas would be successful. She took full responsibility for his education, and worked hard to instill in him a love of reading.

Edison began his working career as a newsboy on the Grand Trunk Railroad when he was only twelve. His day aboard the train was long, and he quickly formed what was to be a lifelong habit; whenever he was not busy, he would stretch out on a wooden bench and have a nap.

Edison also read and studied on the train. He installed a laboratory in the baggage car, and he acquired a printing press and brought out the first newspaper ever published aboard a train.

It was during this time that Edison's ears were damaged for life, but no one is sure just how this happened. There are many stories about it. According to some accounts, Edison's ears were injured when a friend tried to pull him aboard the train. Another story is that the conductor boxed his ears after a chemical fire in the baggage car.

When he was sixteen, Edison became the night telegrapher and station agent at Stratford, Ontario. He quickly got into trouble, partly because he slept on the job and partly because he was involved in too many projects and could not keep his mind on his work.

After he left Stratford, Edison wandered from city to city working as a telegrapher. He never kept a job long, and by the time he was twenty-one, he was considered by family and friends to be a failure. However, he had spent his youthful years learning to experiment without being greatly inhibited by the failures of previous experimenters. He was stubborn, independent, and hard-working, and he began to make his name by creating devices to improve the telegraph. One of the most notable of his early inventions was the quadruplex method, by which four messages could be sent simultaneously over the same wire.

THOMAS ALVA EDISON
1847–1931

As he gained backing, Edison expanded his horizons; soon his inventions included the carbon telephone transmitter and the phonograph.

Edison's incandescent lamp was first demonstrated in 1879, when the young inventor was only thirty-two. Along with the lamp, Edison had developed an entire electrical system.

In the years following this marvelous work, Edison devised a superior storage battery and worked out a way to synchronize motion pictures and sound. Before his life ended, he was to hold more than 1,300 United States and foreign patents. His workshops and laboratories in Menlo Park and West Orange, New Jersey, were forerunners of the modern industrial laboratories where teams of experts try to solve problems, rather than leaving the formulation of new developments to chance and the skill of individual inventors.

Edison became a legend in his own time, and was honored by the distinguished men of science and industry who were his contemporaries. No doubt this delighted him, but what made him feel really fulfilled was the knowledge that because of his tenacity and independence, and his creative ability, the lives of people everywhere were improved and made easier.

The ValueTale Series